Roger Federer

Lerner Publications Company • Minneapolis

Lerner Publications Company
A division of Lerner Publishing Group, Inc.
241 First Avenue North
Minneapolis, MN 55401 U.S.A.

Website address: www.lernerbooks.com

Library of Congress Cataloging-in-Publication Data

Savage, Jeff, 1961–
    Roger Federer / by Jeff Savage.
        p. cm. — (Amazing athletes)
    Includes bibliographical references and index.
    ISBN 978-0-8225-9995-1 (lib. bdg. : alk. paper)
    1. Federer, Roger, 1981– —Juvenile literature. 2. Tennis players—Switzerland—Biography—Juvenile literature. I. Title.
GV994.F43S38 2009
796.342092—dc22 [B]   2008028257

Manufactured in the United States of America
1 2 3 4 5 6 – BP – 14 13 12 11 10 09

TABLE OF CONTENTS

Roger Federer gets set to hit the ball to Andy Murray during their 2008 U.S. Open final.

STILL THE ONE

Roger Federer tossed the tennis ball in the air.
He swung his racket hard and blasted a serve.
The ball shot 126 miles per hour across the net
for an ace.

Roger was playing in the 2008 U.S. Open final. The U.S. Open is the last of four Grand Slam tennis tournaments played each year. More than 20,000 fans filled Arthur Ashe Stadium in New York to see if Roger could keep his winning streak alive. He had already won four straight U.S. Open titles, the most in a row by a male tennis player in the Open era.

Roger concentrates to return the ball.

Roger poses with Andy Murray at the final of the 2008 U.S. Open.

Roger's **opponent** was Andy Murray. Roger played his best in big matches. He never got rattled under pressure. He won by placing his shots in perfect spots. Roger had already won 12 Grand Slam titles in six years. He knew that Pete Sampras's record of 14 titles was within reach. But Roger hadn't won a Grand Slam title in 2008. He came close—reaching two finals and one **semifinal**. Still, some thought Roger's greatness was over. Roger knew better.

Roger easily won the first **set**, 6–2. He was about to take a two-sets-to-none lead. He chased down a shot. He sliced a **backhand** to keep the **rally** going. The ball came back, and Roger smashed a **forehand winner** past Andy Murray. Roger won the second set, 7–5.

Roger hits a forehand to Andy Murray during their U.S. Open final match.

Roger played like an artist in the third set. He chipped **drop shots** in front of Murray. Roger smacked **ground strokes** past him. He scampered across the blue court. Murray had no chance. Roger won the third set, 6–2. He dropped to his knees and screamed with joy. "This is huge," he said after lifting the winner's trophy. "Fans are really supporting me." Murray chimed in, calling Roger the "best player ever."

Roger celebrates after winning the 2008 U.S. Open.

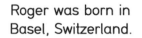

Roger was born in Basel, Switzerland.

EXPECTING TO WIN

Roger was born August 8, 1981, in Basel, a city in northern Switzerland. He grew up in nearby Munchenstein with his parents, Robert and Lynette, and his older sister, Diana.

Roger has been playing tennis since he was very young.

As a young boy, Roger loved hitting a tennis ball. He would watch his parents play at a local tennis court. When they finished their match, they let him join in. Roger was four when he got his first tennis racket. He smacked the ball off bedroom walls and kitchen cupboards. "I banged that ball against anything in the house," he said.

Roger was six when he began playing tennis regularly. By the age of eight, he had joined the tennis club in his hometown. He took group lessons. In 1991, when he turned 10, his family thought Roger was ready for private lessons. They hired Peter Carter, an Australian tennis player, to coach him.

Peter Carter was Roger's coach from 1991 to 1998

Roger was also good in school. He spoke three languages—the Swiss form of German, French, and English. He liked to solve math problems. He played the piano. He was an outstanding soccer player. Roger's biggest passion, though, was tennis.

Roger expected to win. When he played poorly, sometimes he could not control his emotions. He even threw his racket and was kicked off courts.

Roger starred in soccer, but he decided to give up that sport. "I picked tennis because I prefer to be in control of what's happening," he said. "In soccer, if the goalie makes a mistake, everyone pays for it."

In the early days, Roger had to learn to keep his cool on the court.

BREAKTHROUGH MOMENT

Roger didn't want to act childish. He soon learned to control his temper on the court. He focused on playing. At the age of 12, he became the Swiss national junior champion for his age group.

In 1995, at the age of 14, Roger became the junior champion of all age groups in Switzerland. He was chosen to train at the Swiss National Tennis Center in Ecublens. This town is in southwestern Switzerland. He also attended school there.

Roger was eager to improve. But he was lonely. He rode the train home on weekends. He cried every Sunday night on the train back to the tennis center. He graduated from school in 1997 and kept working with Coach Carter. By 1998, he had won the Junior Wimbledon

Roger raises the 1998 Junior Wimbledon championship trophy.

Roger poses with the mascot of the Orange Bowl after winning the Junior Tennis event in 1998.

and Orange Bowl titles. He was named International Tennis Federation (ITF) World Junior Tennis Champion. "I felt on top of the world," he said.

That same year, Roger turned **professional**. He joined the Association of Tennis Professionals (ATP) Tour. His new coach was Peter Lundgren. Roger felt great pressure. After matches, he felt a lot of emotion. Sometimes, he cried after losses. He had trouble sleeping.

Roger competes at the 2000 Olympics in Sydney, Australia.

In 1999, at the age of 17, Roger became the youngest player ever to be **ranked** in the ATP Top 100. He competed in the 2000 Olympic Games in Sydney, Australia. He finished fourth, just missing the bronze medal. At the Olympics, he met Swiss teammate Mirka Vavrinec. They soon started dating.

Roger showed a smooth playing style. He takes long strides to chase down balls. He hits strong shots on the run. In February 2001, he captured his first ATP tournament title in Milan, Italy. Four months later, he was at Wimbledon, England. This is where the oldest Grand Slam tournament is played every year.

In the fourth round, Roger faced the great Pete Sampras. Roger shocked the tennis world by beating him. Roger was thrilled. But a few weeks later, Roger's world came crashing down. He received word that his former coach Peter Carter had been killed in a car crash. Roger deeply felt the loss of his friend. It took him some time to get interested in tennis again.

Roger serves to Pete Sampras at Wimbledon in 2001.

Roger *(left)* and his coach, Peter Lundgren, pose with his Wimbledon trophy in 2003.

GRAND SLAMS

In 2003, Roger won tournaments in France, Germany, and the United Arab Emirates. In July, he was back at Wimbledon. He reached the semifinal round where he beat Andy Roddick.

In the final, he beat Mark Philippoussis in straight sets. Roger returned to Switzerland a national hero.

At the end of 2003, Roger stopped practicing with Coach Lundgren. "I think there is a benefit to figuring things out for myself," he said.

Swiss officials presented Roger with a unique gift in 2003—a milking cow. He named her Juliette.

Two months later, Roger breezed through his opponents to win the 2004 Australian Open, the year's first Grand Slam. In the final, he beat Marat Safin, who said, "I just lost to a magician." With the triumph, Roger became the number one-ranked player in the world. "I never thought I would dominate the sport," he admitted.

Marat Safin *(right)* congratulates Roger after their 2004 Australian Open match.

Roger lost in the French Open, the year's second Grand Slam. But he bounced back to win Wimbledon for the second straight time. "I believe in my talent," he said. "I don't fear anyone anymore." At the 2004 U.S. Open, Roger carved up Lleyton Hewitt in the final to capture his third Grand Slam title of the year. He became the first men's player to win three in one year since Mats Wilander had done it in 1988.

Nearly all professional tennis players have a coach. The coach helps a player study opponents and make a plan to beat them. Roger is so smart that he makes his own plan. "I don't need to sit down and talk about an opponent for an hour," he says. "It takes me basically 15 seconds to come up with a game plan. I know everything I need to know."

Roger *(left)* celebrates after beating Lleyton Hewitt at the 2004 U.S. Open in New York.

His style seemed effortless. He made winning look so easy. Tennis fans everywhere adored him. Roger did not allow the attention to go to his head. "It's nice to be important," he said. "But it's more important to be nice."

Roger *(right)* and Andre Agassi pose with their trophies after the 2005 U.S. Open.

THE FEDERER EXPRESS

Writers named Roger the Federer Express. He was like a fast-moving train that couldn't be stopped. He won his third straight Wimbledon title in 2005. Next, he beat the great Andre Agassi for the U.S. Open title. "He's the best I've ever played against," said Agassi.

In 2006, Roger won three more Grand Slams—the Australian Open, Wimbledon, and the U.S. Open. Later that year, he was appointed to be a goodwill ambassador for the United Nations Children's Fund (UNICEF). It helps children around the world overcome poverty and violence. Roger spent part of the Christmas season visiting an orphanage in India. "I've been lucky in life," he said. "It is

Roger's UNICEF work is important to him. He also started the Roger Federer Foundation. It helps kids in South Africa, where Roger's mother grew up. Roger's longtime girlfriend, Mirka Vavrinec, helps direct the foundation.

Roger spends time with children at a shelter in India in 2006 as part of his work with UNICEF.

important for me to help children who do not have the basic resources they need."

Roger won the Australian Open to start 2007. But on the slippery clay surface at the French Open, he lost. It was his second straight loss to the Spaniard Rafael Nadal in the French Open final. "I can cope with losses much easier than I used to," Roger said. Sure enough, he charged right back to win Wimbledon for the fifth straight time. Not long after, he won the U.S. Open for the fourth year in a row.

In 2007, a picture of Roger was put on a Swiss stamp.

Rafael Nadal *(bottom)* jumps to return the ball to Roger. They are playing their long match at the 2008 Wimbledon final.

He started 2008 by getting to the semifinals at the Australian Open. He seemed worn out and not as sharp as usual. Doctors later found he had an illness that makes people very tired. Roger slowly got better. At the final of the 2008 French Open, he again faced rival Rafael Nadal. Nadal was awesome and easily beat Roger. Later that year, they faced off again in the longest Wimbledon final ever. Roger bounced back from being down two sets. But Nadal kept fighting too. After nearly five hours, Nadal finally won.

The defeat was tough for Roger to take. He called it, "my hardest loss by far." But Roger got past it to look toward the Summer Olympics in Beijing, China. He represented Switzerland. A loss to James Blake kept Roger from the men's **singles** medal round. But he and teammate Stanislas Wawrinka won gold in the men's **doubles**.

Roger was ranked number one from 2003 until mid-2008. Rafael Nadal took over the number one spot.

Roger poses with partner Stanislas Wawrinka and their gold Olympic medals from Beijing.

Fans were wondering if Roger could still win the biggest matches. Roger proved he could at the U.S. Open. He defeated seven opponents during the two-week tournament. He became the first man in tennis history to win five straight titles at two different Grand Slam events. "A lot of people are comparing me to the all-time greats," Roger says. "I love that. It's proof that I made it."

Roger raises his fifth straight U.S. Open trophy in 2008.

Selected Career Highlights

2008 Won fifth straight U.S. Open
Won gold medal in men's doubles at Summer Olympics
Reached third straight French Open final
Reached sixth straight Wimbledon final

2007 Won Australian Open title for the third time
Reached second straight French Open final
Won fifth straight Wimbledon title
Won fourth straight U.S. Open title

2006 Won Australian Open title for the second time
Reached French Open final for the first time
Won fourth straight Wimbledon title
Won third straight U.S. Open title

2005 Won third straight Wimbledon title
Won second straight U.S. Open title

2004 Won Australian Open title for the first time
Won second straight Wimbledon title
Won U.S. Open title for the first time
Named ITF World Champion

2003 Won Wimbledon title for the first time

2002 Won ATP tournaments in Germany and Australia

2001 Won first ATP tournament title in Milan, Italy

2000 Reached semifinals of Olympic Games at
Sydney, Australia

1999 Became youngest
player ever to be
ranked in ATP
Top 100

1998 Named ITF World Junior champion
Won Junior Wimbledon title
Won junior Orange Bowl title
Turned professional

Glossary

ace: a serve that a player is unable to return

backhand: hitting the ball while holding the racket so that the back of the hand is facing the net

doubles: a tennis match in which two-person teams play each other

drop shots: soft shots that barely clear the net

final: the round in which only the top two players or doubles teams remain

forehand: hitting the ball while holding the racket so that the palm of the hand is facing the net

Grand Slam: one of four tennis championships played around the world each year. The events are the Australian Open, the French Open, Wimbledon (in Great Britain), and the U.S. Open.

ground strokes: hits of the ball with a forehand or backhand after the ball has bounced once

Open era: a period in which both professional and non-professional tennis players could compete in Grand Slam tournaments. The era began in 1968.

opponent: the player on the other side, the challenger

professional: able to play in tournaments for money

rally: a long exchange of shots

ranked: given a number based on performance in tournaments. The lower the number is, the better the ranking.

semifinal: the round in which the top four players or doubles teams remain

serve: the hit of a tennis ball that starts each point in a game

set: in a tennis match, a group of six or more games. Men's tennis matches have a maximum of five sets.

singles: a tennis match that pits one player against another

tournaments: competitions in which a series of matches determine the winning players

winner: a shot that is not returned and wins the point

Further Reading & Websites

Drewett, Jim. *How to Improve at Tennis*. New York: Crabtree, 2007.

Labrecque, Ellen. *Roger Federer*. Mankato, MN: Child's World, 2008.

Sanchez Vicario, Arantxa. *The Young Tennis Player*. New York: DK Children, 1996.

Roger Federer's Website
http://www.rogerfederer.com
This is Roger's official website, featuring news, records, photos, fan mail, and other information about Roger.

Sports Illustrated Kids
http://www.sikids.com
The *Sports Illustrated Kids* website covers all sports, including tennis.

United States Tennis Association
http://www.usta.com
The USTA's website provides fans with recent news stories, statistics, schedules, and biographies of players.

Index

Photo Acknowledgments

The images in this book are used with the permission of: © Nick Laham/
Getty Images, p. 4; © Gamma/Eyedea/ZUMA Press, pp. 5, 28; AP Photo/
Charles Krupa, p. 6; © TIMOTHY A. CLARY/AFP/Getty Images, p. 7; AP Photo/
Elise Amendola, pp. 8, 23; © Jon Arnold Images/SuperStock, p. 9; © Roger
Federer Foundation, p. 10; © Hasenkopf/Imago/Icon SMI, p. 11; © Pius Koller/
Imago/Icon SMI, p. 13; © Mike Hewitt/Getty Images, p. 14; © Ron C. Angle/
Getty Images, p. 15; © Lutz Bongarts/Bongarts/Getty Images, p. 16; © Clive
Brunskill/ALLSPORT/Getty Images, p. 17; AP Photo/Anja Niedringhaus,
p. 18; REUTERS/Marcus Gyger, p. 19; © Daniel Berehulak/Getty Images,
p. 20; © Al Bello/Getty Images, p. 22; © STRDEL/AFP/Getty Images, p. 24;
AP Photo/KEYSTONE/Georgios Kefalas, p. 25; © Lawrence Lustig/Express
UK/ZUMA Press, p. 26; © Xing Guangli/Xinhua/ZUMA Press, p. 27;
© Matthew Stockman/Getty Images, p. 29.

Cover: © Ronald Martinez/Getty Images.